BINDWEED

BINDWEED

CHRISTIANNE BALK

Macmillan Publishing Company
New York

Collier Macmillan Publishers
London

Acknowledgments

Some of these poems have previously appeared elsewhere.
Grateful acknowledgment is made to the editors of the
following: *The Iowa Journal of Literary Studies, The
Missouri Review, The Seattle Review, Heartland, Pequod,*
and *Crazyhorse.*

Macmillan Publishing Company
866 Third Avenue, New York, N.Y. 10022
Collier Macmillan Canada, Inc.

Library of Congress Cataloging in Publication Data

Balk, Christianne.
    Bindweed.

    I. Title.
PS3552.A4538B5 1986   811'.54   85-13823
ISBN 0-02-627660-7

10 9 8 7 6 5 4 3 2 1

Printed in the United States of America

BINDWEED

For Mother, For Father,
For Paul

Contents

The Shell

This evening, down
By the river road
I found a shell,
A cicada dead.
His eyes were coral,
And frozen wide,
Bright orange eyes
Stared right at me.
I picked him up,
So the insect sat
Poised on my palm,
As if alive
With olive armor
Hard as bone—
But he was light,
Light as a leaf.

His amber wings
Had two brown spots
Like leaded glass
Stained by smoke.
All black and green
The insect sat
All green with a black
Mask on his face.
And because of the mask
He seemed like one
Who hid his head,
A creature grown old,
Never tired of disguise.
And because of the moon
He seemed to glow
With phosphor inside.

Bindweed

This fence is made of nine-gauge steel diamond mesh,
To keep rabbits and dogs out of the lettuce.
My husband and I built it, so each post
Is thirty inches deep and ten feet apart.
But we didn't plant the vine that weaves
In and out of the chain links, clenching
The wire in tight spirals. It creeps underground
In the stony soil, then springs up. The leaves are sharp,
Pointed hearts. The buds look like miniature pears,
Twisted and bloated and green. After they turn
White as milk-glass, they puff open
Into sky-blue flowers, translucent as bone china.
The petals are fused, and funnel-shaped,
But torn in places like tissue paper. In each
Cup sits the silhouette of a skinny, mauve starfish
With blurred arms. Sometimes I see
Orange-backed, black-bellied beetles coupled
By the pistils, and once a brown wasp burrowed inside
And emerged with yellow powder piled on its beak.
Each bloom lasts a day or two, then goes limp,
As if an invisible torch were held to its rim.
The lips curl down and melt. They seem
To fall inside themselves, and they turn deep salmon,
Suddenly, like litmus paper dipped in vinegar.
I find them on the ground among the leaves,
Ragged, like broken, deflated balloons,
Like cloth fingers ripped from gloves, and abandoned.
I rake them into rows and mounds, and I burn them,
By the southwest corner of my fence.

Elegy

In Wainwright they say the plane went down in the Brooks Range,
perhaps near Porcupine River, or perhaps in the Arctic Ocean;
It was spring, the rivers were breaking up, and the mist settled in
for weeks.
The plane went down in March, when it rains one day and snows
the next;
When the ice fields split into islands big enough to crush ships.
The plane went down in the early spring, when the snow still drifts
in the wind, snow so fine it works into the tightest weave
of a man's coat;
In the north, where the snow is hardened and serrated by winter
winds, where metal sled runners wear out in days, and where
men do not leave heel marks;
In the spring, when the winds begin to drop, when the snow turns
soft and honeycombed, and cannot support a man's weight;
In the spring, when the winds leave, and the insects come, swarms
of insects that can weaken a man until he cannot walk;
In the far north, where magnetic compasses are useless.
Snowshoe frames can be made of metal from plane keels, sleds
built from wings, harnesses woven from shroud lines;
Cloudy streams of fresh water can be found; and salmon, tomcod,
needlefish, and pike caught;
But the Brooks Range stretches from Cape Lisburne to
Demarcation Point, and few of its mountains are mapped.
The plane went down in the north, where valley glaciers crack
into crevasses above deep, granite beds;
In the spring, when rivers swell with melt water, when
snowbridges are swept away, and debris dams up the streams;

In the north, where the overflow fills the flatland with shallow,
   swampy lakes.
Beaver, marmot, and ground squirrel can be trapped; and molting
   spruce grouse, arctic loon, and ptarmigan can be snared.
Bushes can be dug for the starchy roots; cup-fungus, bracken, and
   the inner white bark of willow, poplar, and birch can be eaten;
But the north is filled with rose-capped mushroom, water hemlock,
   baneberry, and amanita.
A plane crashed six years ago in the Bering Sea, in water so cold it
   paralyzed the pilot's hands, but he used his teeth to lash
   himself to a raft with ripcord.
A man went under for forty minutes in the Yukon River, but was
   pulled up breathing because the water had been just cold
   enough.
But masses of sea-ice crowd into the bays in the spring, colliding
   with each other and the coast, and the booming can be heard
   for miles.
A woman lifted an ice-wall in Kotzebue, fracturing her spine, but
   she held the ice up so her husband could crawl out.
A plane crashed near Eagle, and a woman dragged her husband
   from the fuselage, and she melted snow in her mouth, and
   brought it to him, until help came.
A Galena trapper was lost two years ago, but his wife waited, and
   pounded beef suet, berries, and bacon with a wooden mallet
   into pemmican, for his next trip out, and he was found;
But tundra streams wander aimlessly in the spring, and often lead
   to marshes filled with mosquitoes, midges, and blackflies.

The Young Widow Talks to Herself

His absence is a gouge in the snow
Scooped between the spruce trees.
His absence is a hastily-dug hollow
Rough inside and scratched
As if swept by a pine branch.
It is the mark of a pheasant
Who dragged his wingtips
Just before leaving the ground.

Months ago it was tawny canvas,
Laceless, smeared with grease,
Like a shoe lying on a road.
The soles were worn smooth.
It was not stained with blood.
The toe was bent and wrinkled
Slightly, and the upper bulged
As if still filled with a foot.

Once, in a dream, his absence lifted
Like a jet off an asphalt runway.
It shrank to the size of a nighthawk
Before slicing open the clouds.
It disappeared into the sky,
And the hole closed, slowly
Sealing its edges shut.
Only wisps of vapor remained.

But in the morning it was not gone.
It was resting beside a river.
Its outer rim was notched
Like a feather, ivory and ribbed,
And bright, bleached by the sun.
Its shadow lay beneath it
Like another feather, hidden—
Bone-black on the gravel.

Soon it will lay out on the grass.
Leaves will rustle beside it,
As if next to an unhinged door.
They will move into the spaces
Once covered by panels.
Its frame will be broken,
Splintered, as if by a fist.
Pachysandra will grow in the cracks.

Driving Through the Wall

Awake, I see the plaster ceiling,
mottled dry spots on a just-set cast.
Light, sliced by the venetian blinds,
stripes my bed with steel bars,
warm and heavy on my legs.
The broken sun bands the scene
which hangs like a silver-framed windshield,
frozen on this fourth floor wall.
Looking in, I press close
to scalpel-sharp wipers clearing
arcs of amber rain. I see dusk,

low hills draped with sheets of snow.
The pale green road curves
beside fields where farmers plough
around boulders. Revealing just their tops,
the stones are hidden in the dirt.
The road is carving the Minnesota
landscape in two. White lines
unroll, cut exactly in lengths
that lead to my husband's
home town. The road and its gravel shoulders
taper, and end at the underpass;

beyond, I see sedans, pick-up trucks,
fastbacks, and black limousines
moving down the small town street,
crawling to church on Saturday morning.
In the opposite lane, a tractor trailer
roars by, its boom turning into a groan.
A taxi caterwauls around the corner,
brakes, and joins the slow parade.
It is a bright September day
and all the headlights are on.
I hear doors open, and close—

nothing moves. Above the bridge
the sky is streaked with pink:
traces of red on white tile.
I want to see what is not there—
the pile of maps, the thermos of coffee,
my husband beside me.
The venetian blinds sway, dividing
the wall with their slate gray shadows.
Outside the window I see
transparent trees, chimneys,
rooftops, and pigeons flying home.

The Young Widow Studies the Sky

1.
The sky looked just like this the day
He taught me how to step off cliffs backwards.
What did I trust that afternoon? I leaned
Backwards over the Palisades Kepler ledge.
Did I trust the webbed nylon strap he'd wrapped
Around my hips? Or my boots with their gussetted
Tongues? Or the three-strand, five-thousand-pound
Tested rope that belted him to the basswood
And me to him? Below, the stones on the shore
Looked like pebbles. What good would the spun-glass
Helmet have done? I stepped into the air.
For a moment my feet found nothing to kick
Against. Then all I could do was lean back
Against the rope. He lowered me past the wasp
Nests, past the crumbling ledges, past the juniper
Seedlings rooted in handfuls of dirt, past the smooth
Face of rock studded with steel pitons, slowly
Past the tops of the willows and cottonwoods.
I landed beside the river. When I looked
Up, there was just a limestone cliff between us.

2.
We were painting the back porch. We looked up
And saw a small cloud descending on our aluminum
Ladder. We backed down and stood in the driveway.
We even forgot to argue. We just stood there,
His arm touching mine, waiting to get stung.
We could have gone inside. But we just stood
There, with our eyes closed. The swarm surrounded
Us, soft pellets striking our feet, necks, legs,
And faces, whirring like hundreds of metal-edged
Pinwheels. They turned the air into something viscous,
Until it seemed we stood underwater, and then
We were the water, our skins the top of a lake
Pockmarked in a storm. Did I think we were two
Trees whose roots crossed each other so often they'd never
Be hacked apart? We just stood there, watching
Them ripple on the porch roof. They wove themselves
Into a blanket of gray-gold mohair, tailored
Themselves to fit the dovetail joints, the dogwood trees,
And then the sumac. We laughed at the stripes of barn red
House paint smeared on the outsides of our thighs.

Artist's Room

His room is filled with violins and knives,
And scrolls are piled on shelves beside the clothespins.
Each day he mixes jars of beetle resins
With tree gum, purple crystal and amber dye.
He's searching for a varnish to apply
On spruce, to make it deep and opalescent,
A clear lacquer, but strong enough to lessen
The splitting of wood that comes with age and dries
All instruments. Shellac, he says, should be
Like lake water splashed with oil and gasoline;
A lens; a skin encasing Stradivari's
Finest; so pure it burns as anthracite—
Orange, then blue—then gone, illusively
As colors leave a raven's back in flight.

The Holding Rocks

1.
The night we pulled off Upper Crow Ridge
Road. Remember? We parked close to the barbwire
fence to watch the clouds reflect a globe
of light above the city twenty miles east.
Horses walked beyond the fence.
Their tails and legs dark as the trees.
The moon dappling their bodies
with gray light, fusing them to the field.
Their necks low and their noses brushing the grass
as if searching for something they'd just lost.
They stopped and stood next to the car. We heard them.
Breathing. We sat with the engine off and one window open,
letting the air come between us. Nothing moved.
Except the horses scratching the ground with their hooves.

2.

The first time you disappeared I looked for you all
morning all over.   I found your cedar chest
crushed.   The lid caved in, the sides splintered.
Paint tubes twisted, the metal torn, colors
smeared on the dining room floor. I found you in the basement
by that furnace. You scared me. Holding an armful of canvas.
You'd already destroyed two of them. *I want them clean.*
I want the sky to look like lake water splashed
with oil and gasoline. The clouds to burn pure
like anthracite. Orange, blue—then gone, illusive—
as colors leave a raven's back in flight. You asked
me if I remembered the day the welsh mare dropped
her first foal, the day the builders poured
the cement foundation for our house. I said no.

3.

I've seen how quickly colors leave a raven's back,
faster than spirea petals fall when lightly
touched.   Our yard
is flecked, then edged with scraps of white.
What man can hold with two hands all that the sky
carries, cradles, and without warning flings down?
For a while   you mixed oils   stretched   sized
the canvas. Then you stopped. *I want each canvas clean.*
It was May. We hadn't turned the garden.
Hadn't planted, mulched, or fixed fences
for the beans. I took the seedlings out
and slipped the peppers in the ground. Covered them
with plastic to keep the wind away until they hardened.

4.
Remember how cold the air was the day you
showed me where the springs fed into the lake?
We swam like seals with just our heads out. Underwater
our bodies were warm. I followed you, pulling
my legs behind me like an injury through the deep
pool by the raft. My hands stroked the water
as if searching for something we'd just lost.
Past safety buoys, moss-covered ropes, each other's
fingers. I followed you. Away from the cottages,
from ruffled mothers who stood ringing the dinner bells.
Even away from the raft. The bells called us back.
But we kept swimming. We swam hard to reach
the cold spot. Swam to feel the air get yanked
out of our lungs. To feel the air suddenly rush back inside.

5.
The tent stakes were loose in the sand.
I thought they'd hold. *They won't* you said.
You found four empty wire spools and dug four holes
three feet deep. Alone it took you hours. The water
was calm, the sky clear, and I hated you for our wasted
day.   We went to bed.   I remember waking.
Outside the wind was picking up. I moved into your arms.
The sand sliced at the nylon walls. Our ears
ached. We sat inside that bass drum with the sand
slicing at the nylon walls for hours. I thought
we'd never leave. *We will* you said. We crawled
out at dawn. There were trailers on their sides
all along the beach. Piles of bright tents
collapsed. Ours was the only one standing.

6.
All that's left of the barn are two cracked slabs,
warped floorboards, and strands of tangled barbwire.
A torn piece of tin roofing hides the well
fringed with pieces of scarp wall. Remember?
The windows were what you wanted. *The panes*
fogged up in the winter by the cows' heat
and the pony's heat. She was numb, staring down at her
still foal. How quickly you knelt beside them!
You lowered your head, opened your mouth over one
of its nostrils and you sucked and you spit
and you sucked until the foal was breathing by itself.
We rubbed them with empty grain bags and put them
in the west stall to keep the wind away
until they dried. We walked out there your last
night home. Stopping to see the coral portulaca rooted
and blooming in the floor. *Look at what the rocks can hold.*

7.
For years I was sure you'd understand someday
why I wouldn't let you burn any more of your paintings.
Why I made you go. They said the first stroke
was mild but after the second they had to operate
to save your lungs. I stood by your bed and reached
for your hand. I didn't mean to hurt you.
The nurse said it might be like this for weeks.
I just watched you work-over each breath on the other side
of the bedrail slats. All I could think of was the night
the barn burned down. I stayed inside the house.
I couldn't see any flames. All the men
wore masks. All I could see were the silhouettes
of men. Small and soft against a cliff of smoke.

8.
I lied to you twice in that St. Benedict room.
You asked me, again, if I remembered the day
they poured the cement. I said no. I said
I'd dreamed of sitting at a table with two children.
The fourth chair was empty. I told you we waited
while windmills with spokes of red and yellow cellophane
whirled around. Then you walked in and sat down with us.
Even as I spoke I remembered how the building crew
lined the hole with wood and gravel before they poured
the liquid sand foundation in. They built a plywood fence
to keep the wind away until it hardened. I thought:
so this is what we built the frame and walls on.
All our rooms are piled on top of mud and riprap.
The dream? We waited all night. You never walked in.

9.
When you could talk and wanted to I could
not play *remember*. All I could do was bring
you things. Shaved ice to suck. A flat stone
half the size of your palm from the garden.
You held it for days in your left hand before you
died, stroking your fingers slowly over its
white curves. *How can a grazing horse*
see the field in every direction
without raising its head? I didn't know. I
didn't even know they could. It wasn't even me
that thought of bringing you the smooth stone.
It was the nurse. That night I dreamed you lay
on top of me, crushing me with your weight.
I had to use both hands to push you off.

10.

For years I've thought that some late August
day when it was time to pull the bean vines
off, I'd look up and find you standing beside
me. I was sure we'd pull each stalk and branch off
together, then heap them on the mulch pile. I was
sure we'd both look up together and see the bluest eye
we'd ever seen. It would be the first morning glory
in bloom. I thought we'd carefully untangle each tendril.
We would not rip that vine off. We'd move slowly, and when
we were done, the whole fence would be clean. I was sure
I'd see your hands again. But now I can't
face that fence. It's August and I will let the vines
stay. Soon I will tie cheese-cloth over the bent
sunflower heads. To keep the birds from ripping them apart.
This winter, for the first time since you've been gone
I'll do what we used to do. I'll take those sunflower
heads and throw them on the snow
under the pines. For the finches and jays to rip apart.

                                         —For Paul (1953–1979)

The Yellow Hills in Back

I can't tell my husband about the vacant lot
below my fourth floor window, in back
of the Mercy Hospital parking ramp.
Where all the city streets end.
The ground is pale, fawn-brown, and hard—
cracked like a man-made lake bank
cracks before the crown vetch and pampas grass
take root. We talk about his truck. The weather.
Then his truck again. I don't want to talk
about the child I lost two days ago, the second
child I've lost. His children. When I look
at him he looks straight past me, looks
at the wall. As if he were looking down the westbound
lane of Interstate 80 north of Lincoln, Nebraska.
Nowhere near this town. I stare outside
at the trefoil-covered hills south of town,
hills heaped like mounds of sulfur, hills
that slowly blend into the chlorine-colored pastures.
Black cows graze out there. Their calves lie still.
Outside, the catalpa leaves sway and throw
netted shadows on the streets, softening
the edges of the cinder block houses.
The silence settles down on both of us
like a sheet draped on two living room chairs
in a cottage by a lake in late October.

The Top Floor Window

Dawn
The sun is melting frost on the tar paper roof next door,
so it glistens, as if still wet with Chinese-red paint.
From my second-story window, the pitched roof seems to curve
as the low, mottled light of early morning moves
slowly up the ridge pole. A series of shadows on the west slope
of the roof make it seem troughed, like warped plywood.
Some starlings emerge from the long cave below the eaves
to stand on the gutter with puffed bodies, then suddenly
dive down to the lawn, where they swagger beneath the trees.
The wet ground flickers, as if filled with splinters of glass.

Dusk
This afternoon the shadows fall in pleated panels,
like gauze curtains, gray with age, lowering themselves
slowly, between my house and the stucco wall of the house
next door. The pebbled, pockmarked wall is beige, and streaked
with rust, like a great dane's brindle fur. I see a window
across from me, pink as the inside of a Bermuda conch.
The glass turns cinnabar, then sloughs all color off, like water.
It stares for a moment, blind as an empty socket in a skull.
As the wall darkens, the window turns ivory, bright as an exit
of a mine seen from deep within the shaft.

Why Are Young Things Spotted?

Once, when a finch died, mauled by the Persian housecat,
gutted, left still breathing beside the garden
wall: a young boy found the creature spread out,
        opened on shale steps.

Later, nighthawks circled in the barnyard floodlight.
From his window, the boy saw deer jump over the fences.
Lightning bugs flashed in the trees, and he heard cicadas click,
        down by the garden.

Soon the rhododendrons bloomed near the farmhouse.
The boy sat close to the shrubs, asking why dogs
stalk the stream-fed ponds for raccoon and muskrat,
        wondering these things:

Why does the hound pup roll on his back, exposing
his belly, soft as a ripe grouse hung three days dead
from the front porch beam? The hound bitch just sniffs,
        licks at the young pup.

Angry sorrel, smelling the stranger's bay coat:
when the foal's head lifts, and it reaches skyward
with its nose, what stops you? Your hooves are still hard,
        sharp as the field stones.

Greasy starlings, flicked as if with a paint brush,
quickly spattered: how do birds escape night?
Why are young things spotted? So many hues blend
        fawns in the bent grass.

Winter

My father's feet skimmed the pond,
leading me out to the skaters.
Two children and a man whirled,
cutting a circle over and over.
I saw watergrass growing on the bottom.

The man grabbed one child
by her arms and swung her.
Her legs floated off the ice.
She lay flat on the air.
One blade big and one blade small—
they looked like a pair of scissors
spinning wide open
against the dove gray sky.
I wanted to rise like her,
holding onto my father's hands.
The first crack was dull and hollow,
like a gun fired half a mile away.
The man crouched down,
swinging the girl until her stomach
almost touched the ice.
The second crack surrounded us
with white lines. I forgot my father.
All I thought of were my feet,
my feet and some sound stuck
between my shoulder blades. I turned
to him and yelled *come on.*
He seemed farther out than before.
My boots reached the ground.
I held my arms out to him—*come on.*
The ice snapped again, a muffled sound.
He shuffled so heavily, so slowly!

Finally, he stood beside me.
The ice was covered with dark pools.
He took my hand and we walked along the shore.
On the north side we found clumps
of bright green chives growing in the snow.

Falling Men

(John Muir remembers the Merced Face, Sierra Nevada, 1870)

There were no fingerholds. No rifts. No flaws.
Just the 45-foot face I didn't know
how to cling to. I saw myself as two men.
One could let go, bounce down the gully's fractured
steps, fly down towards the snowfield. The other
man saw nothing strong enough to hold his
weight, no crevasse cracks. I looked down
and saw the river paths washed silver
by the snow. In the gravel beds I saw
the Merced and Tuolumne Rivers gather themselves
together. Next to the stream, a one-room cabin.
The boy inside heard pineburs beating on the roof.
I saw I was that boy. Setting the black
book down on the table next to Father's sleeping
arms, I walked out. The mountain's bare base
was streaked white like seastone punished by the sea,
and the peaks rose sharp. Snow piled in pits
on the north side of Merced Peak. The concave bowls
caught the wind and the wind pounded the snow
against the rock, grinding the snow against itself
until the hollows filled with fine white dust.
The wind rolled the snow along the ridge, carried
it up the mountain, over ice-choked gulches,
over lakes lodged in the crater's throat,
all the way up to the peak. Then the wind
let the snow go to the sky. The snow streamed
from the mountain, weaving itself
into white silk knotted like a pennant
to a mast at the peak, unfurling

its fringed edges high above the cabin.
I saw the dark belt of douglas spruce lash
back and forth along the heavy-browed hills.
I heard Father calling me back
inside to recite Joshua, Judges,
Samuel, and Kings, word for word, by heart.
The snow banners thinned into ribbons
of spun glass, long fingers reaching out
to Conness, Lyell, Maclure, and Gibbs
Peaks. Each banner, half a mile long,
glistened bright as the edge of Father's
axe. They reached too far. They turned
into sheer, gauze arms, barely strong enough
to wave. Then they ripped, faded,
and fell. As the wind blew them down I saw
some of the snow turn into mist and escape,
swallowed by the sky. But most was driven
back down into the bossy drifts on the shadowed
side of the mountain, locked back up in the ice
above treeline. And out of the ice I saw a 45-foot
cliff rise and at the foot of the cliff I saw
the small mark of a man floating down
the gorge as if to kiss the glacier's foot.
And at the top of the cliff I saw the other
man hauling himself onto the upper
ledge, panting, kicking, prostrate, and safe—
lifted on wings he didn't know he had.

Father, It Was Not Salt

*(William Bartram, the American explorer-naturalist, left
Pennsylvania in 1774 on an expedition to Florida. He returned four
years later, eager to share his discoveries with his father, the botanist
John Bartram. Arriving home, William found that his father had
died three months earlier. The following are spoken by William
shortly after he returned to his father's farm near the Schuylkill
River.)*

1.
Last week I'd barely put my own
bags down when I learned that you
were gone. I thought of the sharp-shinned
hawk we saw once on the St. Mark Road
not far from Cuscowilla. One wing
free, one wing bound to its side
by the loops of the whip snake wrapped
around its body. The hawk beat
its wing in the yellow dust for hours,
struggling to lift itself off the ground,
fighting the dirt, the air, the knot.
When we came back the next day
all we found were swirls of clay-colored
dirt fanning the sides of the road.
I thought of our first trip thirty
years ago through the Catskills.
Half a mile up the trail I saw
that mound of brown coils rooted in rock,
round as a fungus ear. I wanted
that ear. To bring to you. To show you
mushrooms do grow on Gilian Mountain.
Just as I reached out to touch—
your yell hit me. I saw the ear

uncoil itself, suddenly thick
as a boy's leg and long. Its eyes
were half shut but its tail twitched,
rattled in the air an inch above the ground.
That sound. Your voice. Your breath. Your words
rushing past my ears, neck, scalp—
Stand still. Don't move just yet.

2.
The Schuylkill's in those willows
near the greenhouse. But I can't see
it. How hard I always used to try
to see it. *Rained harder than we thought.*
River's high. I'd stand close to your desk
my shoulders touching yours. Almost
in your lap. All I wanted was
to see what you saw. I'd search each tree,
search for just one glimpse of water.
The willows teased me the way they
tease me now, their leaves pushing
silver currents through the air.
Following my line of sight, you'd catch
me fixed too high and shake your head.
No rivers flow up there. I'd look
down at the desk in front of us.
Unbuckling the strap, your hands
suddenly seemed stronger, bigger.
I'd watch the layers of paper
and the wood slats fall apart
from the press, until the solid box
lay in pieces. Your fingers flicked
the cotton batting apart, opened
the silk-lined paper sheaths and snaked
the *caelistina* petals out. One
wooden press, ribbed with hardwood
sticks, had kept those flowers safe
all the way from St. Juan's River.

3.
Hearing us push through the brush,
they rose on black-tipped wings, wheeling
and circling together, turning
themselves into one giant crane.
I shot four times, breaking them
into a hundred birds. Four fell.
I heard their quill feathers creak
as their wings slapped and cut the air
as if they believed their bones
were strong enough to carry lead.
We heard them hit the swamp. I sliced
the first neck to belly,
then the second. The third one's flags
pierced my hand. I tried to jerk away.
My flinch just pushed the feathers deeper.
It took some time to stop the blood.
Inside the fourth we found two eggs
dropped low, ash-colored, specked with brown,
and ready to be laid. I thought of how
an hour before she'd stood on top
of her stilted nest, wings held out
like tarps to keep the lining dry.
Then I stuck my hands inside her,
curled my fingers around one egg.
I pulled them out, one by one. Father,
you could not stand to watch. But you
were there to pack the wings, the bills, the flags,
the torsos stuffed with grass. And, of course,
the eggs. You wrote your name on every box.

4.
Father, the trout were pewter-skinned,
cast in copper then streaked with slate;
their fins were clematis blue,
their gills were gashes in their heads.
The trader found your letter tucked
in the folds of his mule bag.
I said I'd write you but I never did.
He and I ate broiled trout and rice
cooked with oil and oranges that night.
The snake birds tasted stronger than fish,
too strong to eat. But the yellow
bream was pale, powdered with rust, blue,
silver, and green. A peacock crescent
underlined each eye and it was sweet.
We traded strings of locust-fattened
pied-rice birds for fawn skins filled
with honey. The turkeys tasted just
like acorns. The trader showed me
where the waterbirds nested: bittern,
teal, and duck. Fledglings dressed in cream-
colored down. We used our sticks to bash
their heads, bagged the squabs, then roasted
them with rice. Each chick was nothing
but a mouthful of fat, tallow
softened by the fire. The next day,
crossing the cane swamp, we found a level
clearing, the ground clay-white and carved
with bowls where the cattle lick.
I found one spot not covered with manure,
knelt down, and lowered my face.
I licked the ground. Father, it was not
salt. It was as sweet as hickory

milk. Father, the red-belly fish
were as large as a man's hand. Their heads
were olive green, their sides were pearl
and striped, their flesh was white
and tender, Father, they bit at any bait.

Unresolved Snapshot

The two girls, caught shrugging
Just as the shutter snapped,
Have brown, furry spots
Where their eyes should be.
Their mouths have no openings.
They are shadowy and soft
As if half-dissolved into each other.
They lean toward their father,
Whose arms and shoulders
Surround them like a doorjamb.
Two cloth overnight bags sit
Hunched over on the sidewalk.
Today is the last day of July,
The day the girls go back

To their mother's house.
Their father's face seems seared
By smalt-colored streaks
Thrown, in lines from the trees.
His hair is trampled flat,
Springing up in patches
To poke angry fingers
At the beryl sky,
The livid sky which hangs
Above the three of them.
Behind them, the street tips.
Cars, trees, and houses sit angled,
Askew with the foreground,
Barely balanced on the slope.

The Kitchen Shears Speak

This division must end.
Again I'm forced to amputate
the chicken's limbs; slit the joint,
clip the heart, snip wing from back,

strip fat from flesh, separate
everything from itself. I'm used,
thrown down by unknown hands,
by cowards who can't bear to do

the constant severing. Open and close!
Open and close. I work and never tell.
Though mostly made of mouth, I have no voice,
no legs. My arms are bent, immobile

pinions gripped by strangers. I fear
the grudge things must hold.
I slice rose from bush, skin from muscle,
head from carrot, root from lettuce,

tail from fish. I break the bone.
What if they join against me,
uncouple me, throw away one-half,
or hide my slashed eye? Or worse,

what if I never die? What I fear
most is being caught, then rusted rigid,
punished like a prehistoric
bird, fossilized, and changed

into a winged lizard, trapped while clawing
air, stuck in stone with open beak.

Mother and Child

A child pedals down the street
in an orange plastic go-cart.
The wheels rattle on each crack.
Pieces of torn leaves
lie around me on the lawn.
Yesterday Mother shaped the chinese
privet bush into a perfect box.
Beside me, a line of black spears
points up to the sky.
I lean on the iron fence
and wait for her exit.
The schnauzer hangs from the leash
anchored in her right hand,
his front paws dancing
just above the ground.
"You're choking the dog," I say.
She loosens the rein
and in the silence the dog
lifts his leg on the hydrangea bush.
The wide, low branches lie
on the ground, swayed by the weight
of the white flowers. "Seen
this morning's paper?" she finally asks,
"typist needed on the west side."
I light another cigarette and cross
my arms over the size-large
man's button-down shirt that covers
the child I've carried six months now.
"They let typists nurse
their babies on the job?" I ask.
She reels the leash in,

drags the dog toward her.
"The papers are signed. Don't
let that couple down."
The garage door opens,
the car backs out and she
backs out. "Take out
the garbage cans, okay?
I'll bake chicken tonight."
I watch her car shrink down the road,
sharp and flat as the last tin
target parading inside
a carnival shooting stall.

Instructions from My Mother

Peel the topsheet down. Hold the eyelet hem
    high in the air so it floats
     for a moment
   the way the sound of your father's car floated
    between us this morning.
   Let the sheets fall in a heap at the foot.
  The high knock of his car. Idling for a long time
the way a gull idles in the wind above the water,
        motionless. Release
     the cupped elastic corners on your side.
    Don't worry if it's hard to do—
    fitted sheets are made to hug the mattress tightly.
    There was a surge in the traffic. All
     the cars began to sound like his.
Yank the sheets from their place between the mattress
    and the bedsprings.
        Something keeps the blankets anchored
       tight as ginkgo leaves
      for a while.
     To skin a pillow, grab its lip. Turn
    it upside down so the feather bag falls out
     and the case hangs empty in your hands
like the flour sack we brought home from an auction once
    with all its seams showing.
      Clamp the pillow between your chin and breastbone:
      you'll need your hands. Clean
    cases are hard to get back on.
   Shake the new sheets out. Shake out
     the crushed grass smell

strong as milk from cows let out to pasture for the first
        time in the spring.
                Let them settle by themselves.
            Let the mattress pull the sheets tight around themselves.
            The bedspread isn't straight yet. Tug your side
                so the quilted lines are stitched
                        sharp around us.

Beyond the Farm

Last week he lost
One black retriever
Pup and three chicks.
His shoulder stiffens,
A firm support
For his rifle's stock.

The bird swoops
Centering between the crosshairs
In the telescopic sights.
Just when he feels
The trigger's spring
Resist his finger's pull

He sees the hawk
Drop its scat
Like bits of sheer
Smoke-colored scarf.
He remembers the day
He saw his land

Below, from a Cessna.
Amber and moss patches
Surrounded the barns
Softened by mist
And the gauze-like haze
That grows thicker

Year after year
From the city twenty miles
East, the city blurred
By its own smoke.
Remembering how
The plane jolted

Over invisible stairs
Which only hawks
Maneuver smoothly,
He pauses.
The hawk hovers
Over its own land,

Twisting in the wind,
Cascading, drifting
Flat as silk on air,
As water thins on
Rockbeds, but silent.
It falls, wringing.

He lowers his gun,
Remembering his landing,
How he came down
Loud and lurching
From the plane to plant
His feet on the ground.

Larch Needles

I want to hear anything but the bruised
voice of the black-throated malamute who stands
outside our house this morning. She rests
one paw on a rock and howls up at the sparse
crowns of the larch trees, at their twisted
branch tips and their bent limbs burdened
by strings of sharp, scaled cones. Last October

my father and I stood on the north ridge
of Mount Kennask and looked down at our land.
The larch trees were clouded and soft, an amber
island that marked the family farm among
dark pines. The dog sprinted into the grass,
then stood beside us with her nose pointing up.
A young hawk swung above the phlox-filled ditches,

eyeing the ground for mice. My father sketched
the bell-shaped outline of our land in the air
with his rifle, then wrapped his brown arms
around its stock and said since Mother was gone,
it was just us now. Us, and the house, and the trees
whose branches wove tight above us, whose needles
twisted and draped themselves between us and the sky.

Last January I stopped hunting pheasant with him.
I stopped hiking in the snow with him and the dog.
I don't remember the first time I saw the long,
copper arms of the boy who sat next to me in school,
but I do remember that boy's bare back in April.
He hammered cedar shingles on a roof in downtown Kamloops.
His skin was shiny as polished mahogany in the sun.

Now the dog sees me. She sighs into silence.
But her cry seems to waver near the tree tops.
Two nights ago I told my father I'd be moving
to Kamloops soon to live. For twenty years blue
grouse have fed on the larch leaves that lie as sharp
as glover's needles in a matt around our house,
but in thirty years I know men with chain saws

will come. Our trees will be cut, trucked to mills,
sawed into railroad ties, fence posts, pit props,
and boat masts. Some will stay in Cawston
for snowshoe frames; some will be dipped into sharp
smelling creosote; and some will be sent to the North
Kitimat smelter, where hot slag burns in piles,
without flame, into mud-colored cinder.

The Angst

He sinks from clouds wound
tight around the moon,
from sky to tree to roof,
he swims, he strokes, he dead-man
floats through my bedroom window.
He sings mosquito-like from the ceiling,
drones above the fan.
I never wanted, I never won
this overblown balloon, bloated
boy-shaped carnival prize,
whining in the rafters.
From high above my bed,
he drifts down flat-nosed,
skin stretched tight,
to sprawl, skirling
over me, glistening
like silver plastic,
hovering, helium-filled.
I twist, I turn.
He pules, suspends
himself spread-eagle
then begins to rise
from bed to wall to drapes.
He leaves, scraping
shrilly past the window screen.

Before I Learned to Say Goodbye

I thought the body made its own
morphine. I want you to say to me:
the body makes its own morphine.

You don't hear me. You
don't hear the sound of our skin
on the cotton sheets. Or the scrape
of the metal blade on ice.
You don't know the snow is here.
You reach for me in sleep, pull me
flush against your stomach,
press your knees into the back
of my legs. I'm wrapped in your limbs.
I think it is still falling. I

think somewhere north
of this house a man and a woman
glide along the lakeshore.
They move on bowed strips of wood,
their feet murmuring in the snow.

In sleep your hands
are uneasy. Curving in and out
of me. Restless. Like the horse we saw
in the field east of the lake.
It walked in circles for a long time.
Finally it lowered itself into the gold
grass under the trees.

That couple by the lake—
they can see what's gone.
The snipe-punctured mud-shoals, once
close to the waterway. Leaf
litter. The ruts from mud-dappled,
half-ton pick-ups parked and left on the soft
shoulders with their gunracks empty.
The hollows cupped between grass clumps
in the slough. The silt basins where the herons
stood, stained silver in the early sun. The troughs
gouged in the lake by the cormorants diving,
wings flat against their bodies, slicing
open the water with their bills.
The high-water marks furrowing the shore . . .

It is still falling.
Piling itself on the roof until
it cannot hold its own
weight, sliding
slowly down the eaves, releasing
handfuls of itself into the air,
dropping into the drifts, heaping
against the latticed porch skirts.
Even now the mounds
are filled with dents and holes,
hundreds of holes
sprayed-out and deep as if someone
had emptied a silenced, 10-gauge
shotgun into the snow.

They stand on one side of the fence
watching the dog that sits in the stalk-stubbled
field on the other side. North
of the lake. Howling
with that stretched and broken bark
as if sure he could give both lungs away
if only he could find
something big enough to hold them.
The man wants to get closer
to that dog. But the dog sees the woman
pull one strand of barbwire up in an arch
for the man to crawl under.
Still barking, the dog runs
away from them with his rump low,
tail almost touching the ground,
nose high—
into the frayed edge of forest.

You take my hand, hold my fingers
flat against the left side of your rib
cage. As if to reassure me. As if this
will convince both of us. My mouth touches
yours. Your lips press tight,
closed tight, against mine. This
frightens me. How I don't know
how to make you safe enough.
Opened, you might break.
I feel the cold sweat from your palm
as you press harder.
If only I could reach inside and take
the spots away.
If only I could say *it will be all right.*

Half-awake. You don't want to talk.
Your hands are busy
giving me permission to own tendon,
nail, cartilage, and bone. They say
you will stay here longer. They
take my skin and give it back, oiled
with your skin. They say
the body cannot make its own.

I don't want to hear. I don't
want to hear about the man
who swims in small circles on his back
in bed, his skin
covered with a thin mist of sweat.
His belly stuffed with tumors.
I don't want to hear how he moves
constantly. How he believes he can get
away from the pain.
By moving constantly.
I don't want to hear about those people by the lake.
Or how they've planned to build a six-sided
house in the forest. How he's cut the trees
already, skinned and stacked them.
How he skinned them. Took his knife and slit
the bark along each one. Laid
the dark sheaths back over each one.
To keep the rain off while they cure.
So she will have a place to live.

Can't you see? Too soon we'll want
this moment back. With all its silence.
Too soon we'll step outside in the snow.
We'll walk on narrow, shoveled paths.
Something like the marks left behind by skis
will move between us.

Listen. They are talking.
But with so few words!
A change of wind—*northeast.*
Pellets in the snow—*rabbit.*
Shredded bark—*cedar.*
As if their words don't really matter.
As if they have forever to talk with each other.

How Stories Get Started

You come across tracks. Big, cloven, packed deep
in the snow. The tips of the willow branches
along the trail are nipped off, as if a polite
but famished guest walked by, eating your trees.
The upper twigs are glazed with frozen
moisture from his breath. They glisten in the light.
Clumps of snow are held in the bushes' limbs—
undisturbed nests. Close to your feet a trough
is scooped out where he lay down for the night.
It is as deep as the bathtub in your mother's mother's
house. You lie down in the bottom of the bowl.
You dream of riding something big, unbridled.
Your arms barely reach the sides of its neck.
When you get off and try to touch its face
it steps too close to you and its lips curl
and he smiles at you, like a man you once knew.
He's just a visitor now. Polite, but famished.
The trees aren't enough. He wants to ride
his one-wheel bike with you on his back
on a tightrope strung from tree to tree. You want
to ride but you see what he wants and you run.
Then you can't run. You are buried neck-deep
and your head sways on its stem. Snow trims the barbwire
fence like crocheted lace. Someone has carved
moats in the snow around the base of each willow
and hand-packed the snow against the birch trunks
to keep you from seeing the black parts
of the bark. The bush branches bend
beneath the weight of the snow they hold,

curving over in arches to form snow caves
to shelter you while you sleep at their feet.
You hear someone tall breathing over you.
You hear the scrape of his blade as he digs deep
with his knife to find you. He pulls you out
and yanks out your bones. One by one, he hollows
each bone out, whittling the longest one
into a flute. He presses his mouth against you.

Leaving Sand County:
April 21, 1948

(Aldo Leopold died on this day while fighting a grass fire.)

Under the roughleg
hawk who hovers like a smooth-
feathered bomb waiting

to drop on the marsh,
bare dogwood stems stand exposed
against the hill. I

see men run back and
forth, trying to fight the grass
fire—burning, burning.

Snipe winnow, coots cluck,
white pinions beat the water.
The geese are leaving.

If only I could
stand up now like the others.
Something pulls me up,

flies me north, drops me
above cold, spring-fed streams hemmed-
in by alder. I

pay out more line. Cast
out as the wind swirls the stream,
shaking like a brown

miller. I wade waist
deep through the green cave of tree
branches and the white

throat rolls lazily
in the dark pool as he sucks
feathers down his throat.

The line straightens. I
ease him upstream around each
bend in the river,

slowly, as if I
were the current. I gently
pull him in. Twisting,

as if still swimming,
the trout twists in the wet alder
leaves lining my creel.

If only I could
stay. Here, where only woodcocks
spiral down like stalled

planes. Here, where burn marks
in the grass are covered by
the wide-sweeping arc

of an owl's wings.

Y 6/95